Military Tech

MILITARY GEAR AND SUPPLIES

JULIA GARSTECKI

BLACK RABBIT BOOKS

Bolt is published by Black Rabbit Books
P.O. Box 3263, Mankato, Minnesota, 56002.
www.blackrabbitbooks.com

Marysa Storm, editor; Michael Sellner, designer;
Omay Ayres, photo researcher

Library of Congress Cataloging-in-Publication Data
Names: Garstecki, Julia, author.
Title: Military gear and supplies / by Julia Garstecki.
Description: Mankato, Minnesota : Black Rabbit Books, [2018] | Series: Bolt. Military tech | Includes bibliographical references and index. | Audience: Grades 4-6. | Audience: Ages 9-12.
Identifiers: LCCN 2016049968 (print) | LCCN 2016050334 (ebook) | ISBN 9781680721645 (library binding) | ISBN 9781680722284 (e-book)
Subjects: LCSH: Military supplies–Juvenile literature.
Classification: LCC UC260 .G37 2018 (print) | LCC UC260 (ebook) | DDC 623–dc23
LC record available at https://lccn.loc.gov/2016049968

Printed in the United States at CG Book Printers,
North Mankato, Minnesota, 56003. 3/17

Image Credits

Alamy: 615 collection, 28–29; colin anderson/Blend Images, 3; D. Hurst, 18 (kit); Everett Collection, 18 (right); MICHAEL DUNLEA, 13 (top); Michael Klinec, 10; Nicholas Eveleigh, 18 (food); Roger Bacon / REUTERS, 6 (bottom); shortcut studios, 18 (water), 31; Stephen Barnes, 12; Sunshine Pics, 13 (bottom); US Navy Photo, 6 (full-page); Dreamstime: Alessandroguerriero, 17; Getty Images: arkus von Luecken, 24; Colin Anderson, 26; Scott Nelson, 14 (top); https://www.army.mil/photos: Sgt. Sarah Anderson, 32; Unknown, 4–5; Shutterstock: 3000ad, 1, 8–9, Back Cover; Anatoly Vartanov, 20 (M9); CreativeHQ, 21 (goggles); NEstudio, 14 (bottom), 20–21 (soldier); Oleg Zabielin, Cover; Route55, 18 (bullets); Wikicommons.org: US Army, 23
Every effort has been made to contact copyright holders for material reproduced in this book. Any omissions will be rectified in subsequent printings if notice is given to the publisher.

CONTENTS

CHAPTER 1

Gear in ACTION

Soldiers ride through a war zone. A voice says, "Incoming five o'clock." The driver quickly turns the truck. A bullet flies by.

The voice came from a box inside the truck. It's part of a system called Boomerang. It can tell where people are shooting from.

Soldiers use gear and supplies on battlefields. Gear helps soldiers work. It also keeps them safe.

CHAPTER 2

Electronic GEAR

Soldiers use a lot of electronic gear. They use technology, such as satellites, every day.

Satellites are machines in space. Some of them help find weapons. **Missiles** give off heat when they fly. Satellites sense the heat. They send that information to soldiers. Soldiers can then prepare for attack.

SATELLITES

Soldiers use satellites for different jobs. These machines circle Earth at different heights.

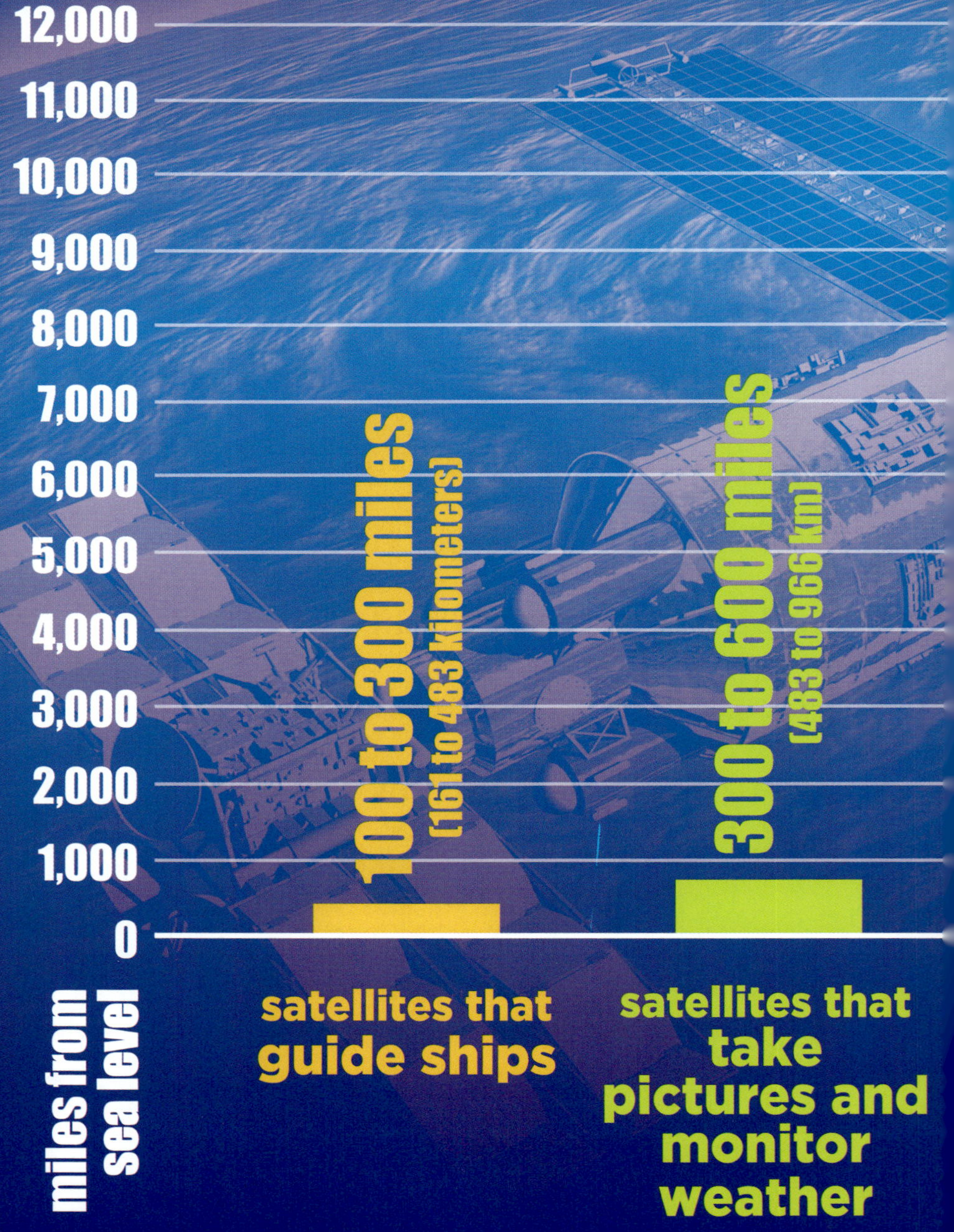

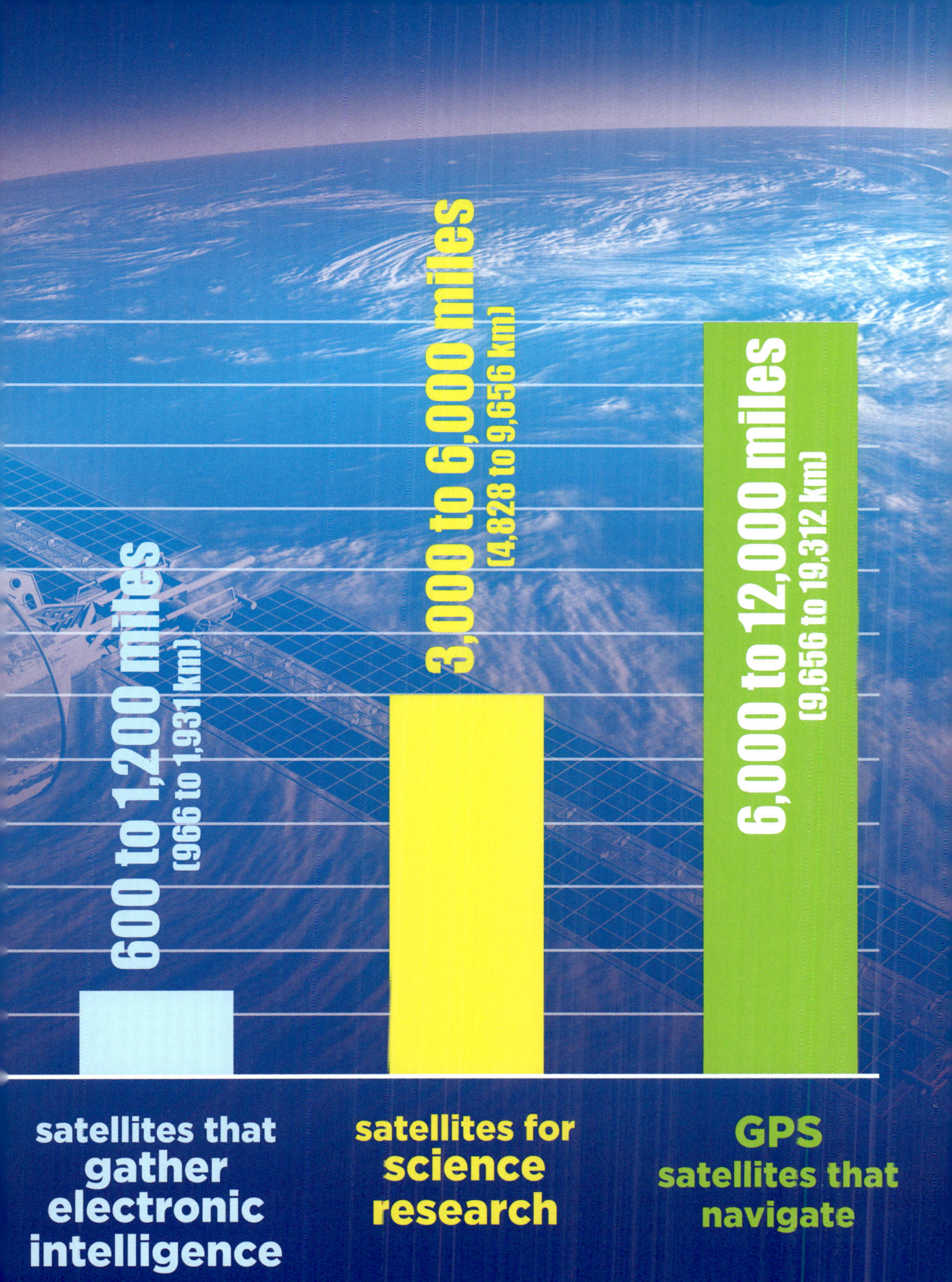
600 to 1,200 miles
(966 to 1,931km)
3,000 to 6,000 miles
(4,828 to 9,656 km)
6,000 to 12,000 miles
(9,656 to 19,312 km)
satellites that gather electronic intelligence
satellites for science research
GPS satellites that navigate

Radar

Soldiers can't always see their enemies. They often use radar to find them. Radar uses radio waves. The waves bounce off objects. The bouncing tells soldiers where objects are. It also shows how quickly objects are moving.

Soldiers carry radar kits. The kits take only minutes to set up. They are helpful in areas full of hiding places. Soldiers use them to prevent **ambushes**.

Jammers

Sometimes enemies hide bombs. A cell phone signal can set bombs off. To stay safe, soldiers use jammers. Jammers' signals block the signals going to bombs. Then **detonators** can't set the bombs off.

Using JAMMERS

SOLDIER COMES NEAR A BOMB

ENEMY SENDS SIGNAL TO BOMB

JAMMER CANCELS OUT SIGNAL SENT TO BOMB

GPS

In bad weather, such as sandstorms, it is easy to get lost. Soldiers use GPS to find their way. GPS stands for Global Positioning System. It tells soldiers where they are.

People use one kind of GPS in their cars. But military GPS is more **accurate**.

CHAPTER 3

GEAR They Wear

Soldiers wear a lot of gear. Their helmets have liners. The liners pump up with air. The air provides cushioning. Cushioning protects soldiers' heads. It helps the helmets fit better too.

Night-vision goggles attach to helmets. This gear lets soldiers see at night. It can **magnify** what they see too.

U.S. Army helmets weigh around 3 pounds (1.4 kilograms).

What U.S. Soldiers Carry

first aid kit

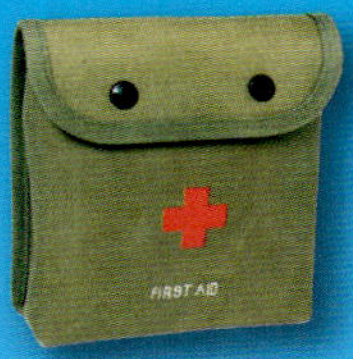

water

ammunition

food

Body Armor

Soldiers also wear body armor. It protects them from bullets and **shrapnel**. Body armor can be heavy. Full armor weighs 30 to 50 pounds (14 to 23 kg). It gives the most protection. But it slows soldiers down.

SOLDIERS' GEAR

M4 CARBINE
KNEEPADS
NIGHT-VISION GOGGLES
COMBAT BOOTS

Airborne Gear

Paratroopers are soldiers who jump from planes. They need special gear. They need parachutes and **harnesses**. They need backup parachutes too. Jump gear weighs around 53 pounds (24 kg). The soldiers don't just have jump gear, though. They carry regular gear too.

Soldiers jump from lower heights than skydivers. They aren't in the air as long. Soldiers must be ready to land right away.

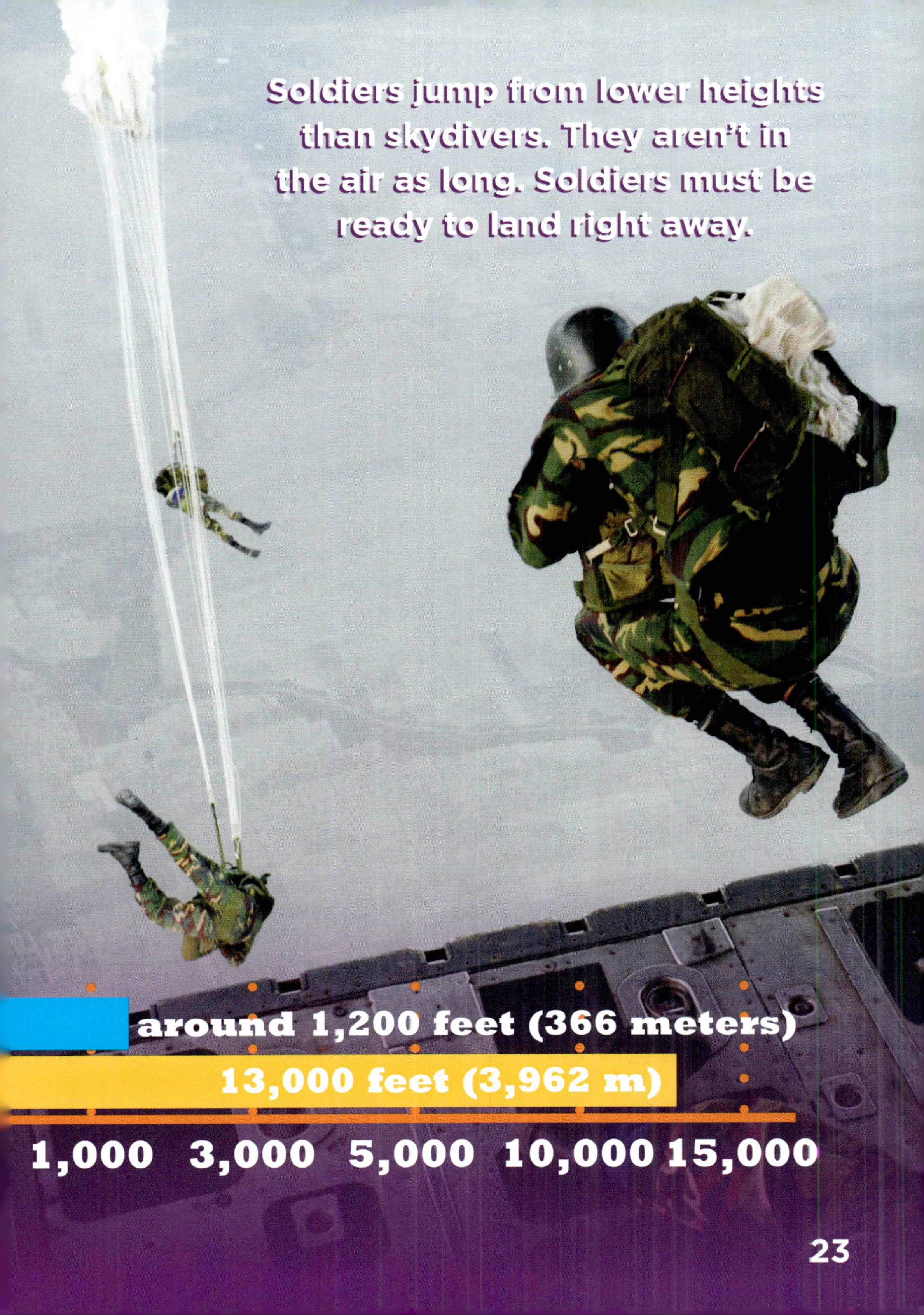

CHAPTER 4

Future GEAR

Scientists are working to make better gear. New gear will protect soldiers. It will make their jobs easier too.

In the future, soldiers might use contact lenses. The lenses could give soldiers super sight. Soldiers could see close and far away at the same time. They could even see what another soldier sees.

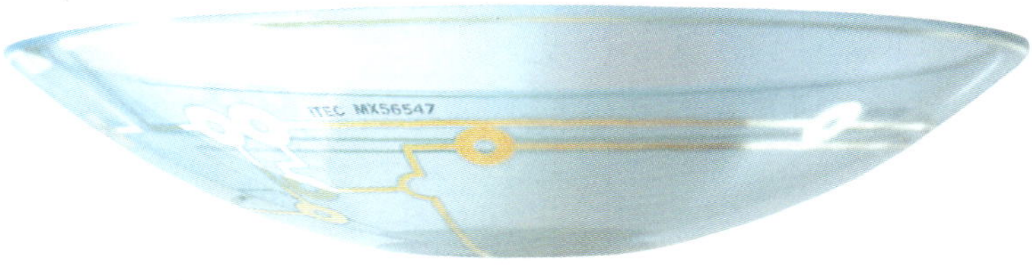

Super Suits

Super suits might be the armor of the future. The suits won't slow soldiers down. They will protect soldiers' entire bodies too.

Scientists are working on these suits now. Some of them have a metal frame. The frame works with a person's body. The frame supports heavy loads.

Constantly Changing

Soldiers use all kinds of gear and supplies. As technology changes, so do their tools. Soldiers learn how to use new gear. Together, soldiers and their gear keep people safe.

SSG DUHART

GLOSSARY

accurate (AK-yuhr-it)—free from mistakes or errors

ambush (AM-boosh)—a surprise attack

detonator (DET-n-ey-tuhr)—a device used to make a bomb explode

harness (HAHR-nis)—a set of straps used to connect a person to something

magnify (MAG-nuh-fahy)—to make something appear larger

missile (MIS-uhl)—a weapon that can be thrown or projected to hit an object far away

sea level (SEE LEV-uhl)—the average height of the sea's surface

shrapnel (SHRAP-nuhl)—small pieces of metal that fly outward from an explosion

LEARN MORE

BOOKS

Bell, Samantha S. *Cool Military Gear.* Ready for Military Action. Minneapolis: Core Library, 2015.

Kassnoff, David. *Special Ops: Weapons and Gear.* Inside Special Forces. New York: Rosen Central, 2015.

Nardo, Don. *Special Operations: Paratroopers.* The Military Experience. Greensboro, NC: Morgan Reynolds Pub., 2013.

WEBSITES

Military Equipment Guide
www.military.com/equipment

Satellite Facts for Kids
www.sciencekids.co.nz/sciencefacts/space/satellites.html

United States Armed Forces
www.ducksters.com/history/us_government/united_states_armed_forces.php

INDEX